HAL•LEONARD
Classical
PLAY-ALONG™
Volume 3

T0082998

Jean Baptiste
LOEILLET
(1680-1730)

Sonata for Alto (Treble) Recorder in G Major, Op. 1, No. 3

ISBN 978-1-4234-6238-5

HAL•LEONARD®
CORPORATION
7777 W. BLUEMOUND RD. P.O. BOX 13819 MILWAUKEE, WI 53213

In Australia Contact:
Hal Leonard Australia Pty. Ltd.
4 Lentara Court
Cheltenham, Victoria, 3192 Australia
Email: ausadmin@halleonard.com.au

Visit Hal Leonard Online at
www.halleonard.com

PREFACE

The Hal Leonard Classical Play-Along™ series allows you to work through great classical works systematically and at any tempo with accompaniment.

Tracks 2-5 on the CD demonstrate the concert version of each movement. After tuning your instrument to Track 1 you can begin practicing the piece. Using the Amazing Slow-Downer technology included on the CD, you can adjust the recording to any tempo you like without altering the pitch. (Note that when using Amazing Slow-Downer, the CD will stop after each track instead of playing continuously.) The full cadenzas are played only in the orchestral version.

- Track No. ⬚1 – tuning notes
- Track numbers in circles ◯ – concert version
- Track numbers in diamonds ◆ – play-along version

CONCERT VERSION

Manfredo Zimmermann, Alto (Treble) Recorder

Mechthild Winter, Harpsichord

Steffen Hoffmann, Cello

SONATA

for Alto (Treble) Recorder in G Major, Op. 1 No. 3

I ②

J. B. Loeillet (1680 - 1730)

3

IV ⑤

Dal Segno al Fine